Epiphany

Six Sermons for a Strange Season

D1361871

By Dr. Chris George

Dedicated to

Dr. Jim Barnette

He was my mentor, my role model, my colleague, and most of all my friend. His sermons were engaging, but it was his way of life that truly inspired me.

Acknowledgements

"Epiphany: A Different Way" was a series of sermons preached at Smoke Rise Baptist Church in Tucker, Georgia during January and February 2021. While the sermons were delivered from the pulpit, the pews of the church were empty due to the Covid-19 pandemic.

The collection of these sermons in written form for publication required significant editing work. I want to express appreciation and give credit to Clarissa Strickland, Mike Jones, Celeste George, Jennifer George and David George for their assistance in this process. Any errors which remain in this text are exclusively mine.

Contents

Introduction

Epiphany represents the most overlooked and underappreciated season in the church calendar. The placement of this season, between the ever popular Advent/Christmas and the absolutely essential Lent/Easter, leads to it being overshadowed by both celebration and contemplation.

Epiphany arrives after the angels have finished their song and the presents have been opened. Epiphany arrives before the ashes have been placed on our foreheads. So, Epiphany's arrival is often unheralded in even the most liturgical traditions. In my own Baptist tradition, Epiphany is simply ignored in a large majority of our churches.

Epiphany is like so many of the beautiful states in the middle of the United States like Arkansas, Kansas, and Oklahoma. We may often travel through Epiphany, but we never travel to it. But, this season is more than merely a banal bridge between more popular liturgical destinations. It is an essential journey that helps us to understand what has taken place at Christmas and prepares us for what will take place on the road to the cross. Epiphany connects the most important universal elements of the human experience.

It begins soon after Jesus' birth and ends with the road to his death. Epiphany is the blessed and beautiful, dangerous and daring, mundane and miraculous in-between time where life happens. Our eyes are opened to new realities and we gradually begin to see more clearly.

It starts with a star in the night sky. A light piercing the darkness.

Those magi who saw the star long ago were inspired to take a trip to an unknown destination and, in the journey, to face birth and death. It was a transformative encounter.

T.S. Eliot wrote in *The Journey of the Magi*:

...were we led all this way for
Birth or Death? There was a birth, certainly.
We had evidence and no doubt. I had seen
birth and death.
But had thought they were different;...

We returned to our places, these Kingdoms,
But no longer at ease here...

Perhaps, the purpose of Epiphany is to awaken us from our post-Christmas slumber and to challenge us to be changed. Birth and Death collide in this season because our lives are meant to be shaken up, so that we do more than merely exist but instead embrace our journey. If we emerge from this season unchanged, then we have never really experienced Epiphany.

Ultimately, Epiphany is an invitation. We can accept it or reject it.

Be warned. Those who accept will be required to travel a different way, hard and holy.

— Chris George

Home by a Different Way

In the time of King Herod, after Jesus was born in Bethlehem of Judea, wise men from the East came to Jerusalem, asking, "Where is the child who has been born king of the Jews? For we observed his star at its rising, and have come to pay him homage." When King Herod heard this, he was frightened, and all Jerusalem with him; and calling together all the chief priests and scribes of the people, he inquired of them where the Messiah was to be born. They told him, "In Bethlehem of Judea; for so it has been written by the prophet:

"And you, Bethlehem, in the land of Judah,
  are by no means least among the rulers of Judah;
for from you shall come a ruler
  who is to shepherd my people Israel."

Then Herod secretly called for the wise men and learned from them the exact time when the star had appeared. Then he sent them to Bethlehem, saying, "Go and search diligently for the child; and when you have found him, bring me word so that I may also go and pay him homage." When they had heard the king, they set out; and there, ahead of them, went the star that they had seen at its rising, until

*it stopped over the place where the child was.
When they saw that the star had stopped,
they were overwhelmed with joy. On entering
the house, they saw the child with Mary his
mother; and they knelt down and paid him
homage. Then, opening their treasure-chests,
they offered him gifts of gold, frankincense,
and myrrh. And having been warned in a
dream not to return to Herod, they left for
their own country by another road.*

-Matthew 2:1-12, NRSV

We've been talking a great deal about
Epiphany this year—perhaps more than in
years past. Some of you have questions such
as, "Exactly when is Epiphany?"

My answer comes: "Now. It is now." Actually,
Epiphany began on Wednesday, January 6, at
the end of the 12 days of Christmas. Did you
know that was more than just a song? In the
liturgical Church calendar, Christmas is a
12-day season. Technically, Epiphany begins
on January 6th. However, Protestant churches
typically begin the celebration on the Sunday
before. So, we are now in the Season of
Epiphany.

The observance of Epiphany, also called "Three Kings Day," is associated with the coming of the magi.

Howard Thurman, African American theologian, provides a thoughtful explanation of Epiphany:

When the song of the angels is stilled,
When the star in the sky is gone,
When the kings and princes are home,
When the shepherds are back with their flock,
The work of Christmas begins.

So, we might say that Epiphany is when the work of Christmas begins.

What exactly is Epiphany?

Epiphany is the season between Christmas and Lent. At Christmas, we celebrate the fact that the Light of the world has come and, during Epiphany, we ask what that means and why it matters.

Maybe you are unfamiliar with Epiphany. Many Baptists are.

Perhaps, this will help. There are at least three different kinds of people in the world. One kind LOVES to prepare for a party or a big event. A baby shower or themed birthday party is like a dream come true. They like to pick out the colors and decorate the tables and make all the behind-the-scenes plans. These folks are often, but not always, introverts and often, but not always, Type A personalities. My wife is one of these people. She loves the checklists and plans. These are the Advent people; Advent is all about preparation.

The second kind of people LOVE the party itself. They lose their patience in the process of preparing. They are not as concerned with color palates and creative ideas. They just want to be at the party—to eat, drink, and be merry. They want to get to the actual experience. These folks are often, but not always, extroverts and often, but not always, Type B personalities. I am one of these people. I struggle with little details and making plans. These are Christmas people — Christmas is all about the celebration.

Of course, after the party is over, when everyone has left, your house is a wreck. The banners are becoming detached from the ceiling, the balloons are losing air and the half-eaten plates of food must be cleaned up. We need people, post-party people, who are willing to clean up. But those people are few and far between...We have the planners and the partiers, but we don't have many folks who are just "chomping at the bit" to clean up after the fact. This is Epiphany - the after-party.

And for this reason, Epiphany is often overlooked and overshadowed by Advent, Christmas, and Lent. Epiphany happens every year, but if we are not careful, we ignore it.

But, I am going to argue, Epiphany is maybe the most important season of all. In Epiphany, we make sense of what has happened during Advent and Christmas, and we prepare for what is to come at Lent and Easter. We are on this vital bridge and if we don't walk across it, we cannot connect these two sides.

So we must not skip Epiphany, but embrace it, beginning today.

We have read the familiar narrative about the wise men, or magi. We have seen those figures in our nativity scenes, so we tend to skim over this event without paying much attention. In short, we treat the story just like we treat the entire Season of Epiphany.

But, if we stop and listen, we may discover something unexpected and important at the end.

The wise men follow the star. They encounter evil King Herod who tells them, "Go. And when you have found the baby, bring word to me that I may go and worship him." The magi find the baby, offering their gifts of gold, frankincense, and myrrh.

We know the story. But notice the last line – that very last line:
Warned in a dream not to return to Herod, they went home by a different way.

Did you notice that? They took another route.

My buddy, Mike Jones, who is a member here at Smoke Rise, has an odd habit. To be honest, he has lots of odd habits. (He prides himself on having more "issues" than *National Geographic*.) But this habit that I am speaking about involves taking a different way home. Mike says, "People who know me know that I do not like to take the same path twice. Always return a different way than you arrived, I say." So, when I ride with Mike to the airport, we go there one way and return by a different way, an alternative route. He does this, even if it takes longer.

The wise men did the same thing. It wasn't to be more efficient. Of course, it made sense, after their dream. But it also made sense, after their experience. For, you see, they were different people. They had been changed.

The story of the magi is really a story about how their experience shaped them and about how our experiences shape us.

Epiphany reminds us that God still inspires us, often using our experiences. God is not trapped back in the story; God is not left in the manger. God meets us in our experiences, and shapes us, making us into the persons we are called to be.

Peter Gomes, a theologian and preacher at Harvard University, writes, "Christian growth is not simply a matter of the *quantity* of time, but the *quality* of that time...Christian growth seems to be a willingness to expose oneself to new ideas, to widening opportunities, to new awareness of what's happening in the world around us...Christians need to grow and mature in their experiences."

And those magi must have done just that. They left the comfort of their homes, departing from Persia. After passing through a great distance, they arrived at the most unlikely of destinations, Bethlehem. They went to this seemingly God-forsaken place— but no, this *God-remembered* little town. It was a place, an experience, that would be so easy to overlook—a peasant couple and their newborn baby that must have looked like everyone else. And yet, this experience changed them and transformed them.

We must not overlook the little things. Listen. God is speaking through our experiences.

Epiphany comes to change us. It is during the season of Epiphany that we talk most often about our baptism. We as Baptists believe that baptism is the outward sign of our inward change.

Kyle Matthews has written a wonderful song entitled, *Been Through the Waters*. It tells the story of a little boy who has been baptized in a river, or creek or a lake. After his baptism, he runs home, not realizing he has forgotten his shoes. His parents poke fun, but the little boy says, "No, I've been through the waters and you don't put old shoes on your brand new feet." Because baptism is a reminder that we've been changed.

Epiphany comes as a season to change us. Ironically, almost paradoxically, it helps us to remember what we have forgotten and to see for the first time what we have failed to see. Somewhere, along the way, we are changed, transformed. We cannot take the same old roads home. We were never meant to take the same road home.

Have you ever tried it—taking a different route? Some of you know that I grew up in St. Louis, living there for nine years, from the age of five to 14. It has always held a special place in my heart. When the Cardinals are playing the Braves, it's always a problem for me; I'm torn in two. I remember my house in St. Louis. I can tell you the address and I can tell you my first phone number. It was a two-story house on Country Ridge Road. A few years ago, I was excited to go back there. And the house is still there; but let me tell you, you couldn't get there the same way. All the roads had been changed; there were new developments, highways, interstates, and detours. I nearly got lost just trying to get to my own house. I finally arrived; but I had to take a different way. I missed the old roads that I had ridden my bike down; but they were no longer viable or visible. I could have mourned their loss, but then I would never have found my home. So, I learned a new way.

It would have been easier and more efficient for the wise men to go home by the way they had come.

It is easier for us to do what we have always done. Change is hard. We've all seen it play out in front of us, in this Covid crisis that has caused us to change so much. Change takes courage. Fear rejects change, but faith embraces it. In fact, our Christian faith was born in it. Don't you remember the story? Death is turned to life because of Jesus' resurrection. And the despair of the cross is transformed into the hope of salvation. Darkness has been defeated by the light. Jesus has changed everything.

Christmas is easy. Epiphany is hard. But God calls us just as he called those magi to take a different route. You see, God cares most not about where we travel, but about who we are becoming on the journey.

Worship is one of those things that should shape us and change us. That's why I'm so glad you are worshiping with us today. John Killinger says, "If we come to church and go home and everything looks the same, it has been a pointless exercise. Things should look different after we have been worshiping the Lord."

We should journey home a different way, because we have become different people.

It is not merely the road you travel, but the way that you travel on the road. It is not merely about where you are going, but how you are going to get there.

The journey led the magi to that little town, to the manger, and to an encounter with Christ.

Our journey leads us to here, to our table, to a time of communion and to an encounter with Christ.

You cannot encounter Christ without being changed.

Let's pray.

A Different Way of Hearing

Now the boy Samuel was ministering to the Lord under Eli. The word of the Lord was rare in those days; visions were not widespread.

At that time Eli, whose eyesight had begun to grow dim so that he could not see, was lying down in his room; the lamp of God had not yet gone out, and Samuel was lying down in the temple of the Lord, where the ark of God was. Then the Lord called, "Samuel! Samuel!" and he said, "Here I am!" and ran to Eli, and said, "Here I am, for you called me." But he said, "I did not call; lie down again." So he went and lay down. The Lord called again, "Samuel!" Samuel got up and went to Eli, and said, "Here I am, for you called me." But he said, "I did not call, my son; lie down again." Now Samuel did not yet know the Lord, and the word of the Lord had not yet been revealed to him. The Lord called Samuel again, a third time. And he got up and went to Eli, and said, "Here I am, for you called me." Then Eli perceived that the Lord was calling the boy. Therefore Eli said to Samuel, "Go, lie down; and if he calls you, you shall say, 'Speak, Lord, for your servant is listening.'" So Samuel went and lay down in his place.

Now the Lord came and stood there, calling as before, "Samuel! Samuel!" And Samuel said, "Speak, for your servant is listening." Then the Lord said to Samuel, "See, I am about to do something in Israel that will make both ears of anyone who hears of it tingle."

-1 Samuel 3:1-11, NRSV

What do you do if you can't hear? This was a question I faced recently.

A couple of years ago, on a Wednesday night— you know, B.C. (before Covid), Smoke Rise was hosting hearing tests in our church's library. We brought in an audiologist to do some preliminary assessments for anyone who was interested. I didn't really need a test and had not planned to have one, but the folks in the library looked so lonely that I stepped in for a consultation.

I put on those headphones that are anything but cool. They make a fashion statement, just not a positive one. And I'm listening for these beeps and I am raising my hand, as any of you have been tested remember. I finished the test and prepared to get the good news. Then the audiologist tells me, "Your hearing is good, but not great."

I learned forward and said, "Now what did you say?" He repeated it more loudly and slowly, "YOUR HEARING IS GOOD, BUT NOT GREAT." He explained that I would have trouble hearing some consonants and trouble with higher-pitched voices like those of females.

Well, I was feeling a little deflated as I came back to my table at dinner in the Fellowship Hall. I was trying to recount to my family all that the audiologist had concluded by saying that he had told me that I had "trouble hearing female voices." My wife Jen, without missing a beat, said, "Yes, I can verify that."

But what if you cannot hear God speaking? What about those moments in life when, to quote 1 Samuel, "the word of the Lord is rare"?

Most of us are familiar with the kind of difficult experiences of life that some call a "wilderness experience." For some, at these times, silence comes like a season—winter, with blustery winds and bitter cold. It may happen when we experience the death of a loved one. After the visitation and the funeral are over and when family and friends have left, we are alone in a house that no longer feels like home. And the silence is deafening.

That same silence descends in the doctor's office just after the devastating diagnosis. Or in the home of a hopeful mother after a miscarriage.

During this strange past year, many people have struggled with the silence and stillness. They tell me in our phone conversations and read their words in texts and emails. "I have never felt so alone. This place is empty. I just wait and wait. I try to watch TV, but then turn it off and sit in the silence."

Yes, for some it is a season. Of course, for others, silence is an almost constant companion. It was for Mother Teresa, reminding us that even the most faithful among us sometimes struggle with silence. It was her spiritual advisor that shared that for the last 40 years of her life, she wrestled with the silence of God. Mother Teresa wrote, "As for me, the silence and the emptiness is so great, that I look and do not see; I listen and do not hear..."

Now...the word of the Lord was rare in those days; visions were not widespread. -1 Samuel 3:1

These opening lines from Samuel's story do not seem to describe a one-time occurrence, but an event that happens over and over in the lives of those seeking to follow God. But before we get to those words, let us look at the images in this passage, for they are powerful.

Eli, whose eyesight had begun to grow dim so that he could not see... The first image is of an aging priest, living in the shadows. And the image is one of darkness and despair.

But the lamp of God had not yet gone out... That may be the most important verse in the entire story. While it does not break the eerie silence, the lamp does pierce the darkness. It is not yet a word to be heard, but it is an image that evokes hope.

And friends, no matter how deep the darkness and how empty the silence, the lamp of God has not gone out. It was Martin Luther King, Jr., whose birthday we celebrate tomorrow, who once said, "God is still around. And one day, you're going to need him. The problems of life begin to overwhelm you and disappointments will begin to beat at your life's door like a tidal wave. And if you don't have a deep and profound faith, you aren't going to be able to make it. I know this from personal experience."

Hannah, Samuel's mother, knew it too. Oh, she knew the feeling that the word of the Lord was rare. She struggled to conceive, and she prayed over and over, day after day, month after month, year after year. Hannah prayed and cried. She would go out by herself and cry. It's not a bad practice, when it feels like God is silent.

Carl Hart, former member of Smoke Rise and a teacher in the Seekers Sunday school class, remembered, "When I was about 16-years-old, I walked into my mother's bedroom and found her crying. I asked, 'What's the matter?' It was Clifford, my oldest brother. He was off in the war. She had not heard from him in over a month. He was her first son and had been sickly as a child. Without her consent, he had joined the Navy. The last letter she received from him told her that he was in the Pacific. She read news reports after news reports and she just could not hold back. She had to find a place to cry; and so she went to her bedroom and closed the door."

Carl concludes, "I didn't stop Mama from crying. She needed to cry, and so did I." Carl did. And we do. And so did Hannah. God never condemns her for her tears, but instead accepts her prayers and those tears as an offering.

And Samuel, whom we read about in today's text, Samuel is the answer to her prayers. As a young boy, he is asleep in the temple. Then, God speaks. At first, Samuel doesn't recognize the voice. He assumes it is the old priest, Eli, who is calling. And so we learn: Sometimes when God speaks, we don't recognize the voice.

This may be the hardest part of hearing God— learning to listen to the little things that seem insignificant.

Here is what we discover from this story: Sometimes God's voice sounds just like a human voice. Samuel thought it was Eli. God must have sounded like Eli.

Isn't that amazing? But you know it is true that God speaks through human voices.

Most of us have never heard God say, audibly, "I love you." God speaks through mothers and fathers, grandmothers and grandfathers, a spouse, a child, or a friend saying, "I love you to the moon and back. I love you forever and like you for always. I do!" Sometimes, we hear the voice of God through someone who chooses to give you that most precious gift— the gift of their time.

Have you ever heard the voice of God? I have, through family members and countless friends who are on this journey through life, many who are hearing my voice today. Through people in this church congregation, this gathered body. I treasure the wise sayings, even of those, like grandparents, who have gone before us. I can still tell you the words that were spoken by my seventh grade Sunday school teacher.

So many voices calling my name, "Chris, Chris!" At the time, I didn't realize it, but later, looking back, I realized that the Divine was speaking through these human voices.

The voice of God? I've heard it when I read the words of C.S. Lewis and Fred Craddock and Anne Lamott and Peter Gomes and Martin Luther King, Jr. and Barbara Brown Taylor. I hear it when soloists or choral ensembles lift their voices. I hear it when I sing from our hymnal.

Celtic Christians used to talk about "thin places" between Earth and the eternal, little cracks and crevices where the eternal sometimes spills into our world into casual conversations over a cup of coffee. We get glimpses of heaven and find ourselves engaged in a divine discourse wherever we are—on the back porch, or at the table at McDonald's, or on the bridge over the stream.

We are standing on holy ground. It happens.

I don't want to minimize that sometimes the words of books or hymns, or even the heartfelt words of family and friends still seem to ring hollow. There are times in life when "the word of Lord" seems rare. And what are we to do in these moments?

I recently received an email from a church member who was distraught by the diagnosis of a member of her family. She was asking for prayers, but she confessed that she struggled with what to say or how to pray. She couldn't find comfort or sense God's speaking in the midst of this struggle.

What she was saying is, "I am scared, and it seems that God is silent."

Eli might have felt this way. His vision was dim. His hearing was failing. He may have felt abandoned by God, judged and found lacking. He was going through the motions of faith, even if his heart was no longer in it. It must have been hard. But notice, Eli still had a part to play in God's plan.

Eli had not heard God's voice. The story never tells us that Eli ever hears God's voice. But it is Eli who offers assistance to Samuel. It is Eli who serves as God's instrument. It is Eli who tells young Samuel, "Go, lie down; and if he calls to you, you shall say, 'Speak, Lord, for your servant is listening.'"

Eli can't hear, but he can still help. And Eli teaches Samuel to hear a different way.

In those moments in life, even when we cannot hear God's voice ourselves, we may still help others.

It was a couple of years ago, right at this time of year, when I made a New Year's resolution that I would exercise. Most days, I ran a lot and walked a little, maybe a mile total. On many of those days, my son David walked with me.

I don't remember, maybe it was late January or early February, but I got very sick. I was completely miserable, lying in bed. On one of those afternoons, David came to my room, bringing me some Gatorade, and said, "Daddy, I know you're sick. So, I ran for you a lot, because I knew you couldn't." It was like a gift that he had given me.

Of course, exercise doesn't work that way. You can't burn someone else's calories. But, faith works differently.

Do you remember the story of the paralytic man and what happened to him in Mark 2? The man was paralyzed; he couldn't do anything! He is with his friends, waiting to see Jesus. But the room, the house, is so crowded that they can't get in. So, they climb up onto the roof, tear it apart and lower their friend down before Jesus. Now that's an exercise in determination! But what's more amazing is what Jesus says to them. When Jesus saw their faith, the faith of his friends, Jesus looks at the man and says, "Son, your sins are forgiven."

You see, when I can't pray because I don't know what to say or because I am so broken-hearted or disappointed that I can't close my eyes and open my heart or utter a word, someone else says, "I know you can't. Not now. So, I prayed for you; I went to God on your behalf. And I prayed a lot because I knew you couldn't. Not now."

When I cannot believe because doubt has the day, someone else may say, "I know that today it is too hard for you to believe anything, so I will believe for you, and walk alongside you."

Even when you are unable to hear God, you can still help someone else. You can still serve as God's instrument.

Do you need proof? Look at Eli. Look at Mother Teresa. And look at the friends of that paralytic man.

Perhaps I can't hear God now, but I can still help.

We must never forget—God speaks through human voices. We have to embrace a different way of hearing. Because, one day, someday, not far from now, not far from where you are, God will want to speak. And God will borrow a voice. And it will be yours.

Let's pray.

A Different Way of Being

Jonah began to go into the city, going a day's walk. And he cried out, "Forty days more, and Nineveh shall be overthrown!" And the people of Nineveh believed God; they proclaimed a fast, and everyone, great and small, put on sackcloth.

When God saw what they did, how they turned from their evil ways, God changed his mind about the calamity that he had said he would bring upon them; and he did not do it.

But this was very displeasing to Jonah, and he became angry. He prayed to the Lord and said, "O Lord! Is not this what I said while I was still in my own country? That is why I fled to Tarshish at the beginning; for I knew that you are a gracious God and merciful, slow to anger, and abounding in steadfast love, and ready to relent from punishing. And now, O Lord, please take my life from me, for it is better for me to die than to live." And the Lord said, "Is it right for you to be angry?" Then Jonah went out of the city and sat down east of the city, and made a booth for himself there. He sat under it in the shade, waiting to see what would become of the city.

The Lord God appointed a bush, and made it come up over Jonah, to give shade over his head, to save him from his discomfort; so Jonah was very happy about the bush. But when dawn came up the next day, God appointed a worm that attacked the bush, so that it withered. When the sun rose, God prepared a sultry east wind, and the sun beat down on the head of Jonah so that he was faint and asked that he might die. He said, "It is better for me to die than to live."

But God said to Jonah, "Is it right for you to be angry about the bush?" And he said, "Yes, angry enough to die." Then the Lord said, "You are concerned about the bush, for which you did not labour and which you did not grow; it came into being in a night and perished in a night. And should I not be concerned about Nineveh, that great city, in which there are more than a hundred and twenty thousand people who do not know their right hand from their left, and also many animals?"

-Jonah 3:4, 5, 10 and 4:1-11, NRSV

Jonah and the whale may be one of the most familiar stories in all the scriptures. As children, we heard the story in Sunday school; we listened with our eyes wide open, with awe and wonder, at a tale about a man being eaten by a big fish, then spit back up on the beach.

As adults, we began to question some of the details, struggling to reconcile the story with our understanding of science.

And yet, the story is not written to challenge and change our understanding of science, but rather to challenge and change our understanding of God.

Although the story of Jonah is familiar, our scripture reading may sound strange to most of us. In our traditional telling, we typically leave off the this rather unpleasant ending. We talk about God's call to Jonah, then Jonah's running from the call. We talk about Jonah being swallowed by a big fish, then spit up on the seashore. Then, Jonah answers God's call, the people repent, and we assume everyone lives "happily ever after."

Except, they don't.

It is somewhat ironic that we never read that part of the story, because it is the part most like our own stories. Few of us have been called to go to a city and tell of the impending doom. And none of us have been eaten by a whale. Yet, these parts of the story are familiar to us even though these are the parts most foreign to our own experience.

In the verses we read today, Jonah does what God wants, but Jonah doesn't get what he wants.

Now that has happened to all of us at some point or another. Like Jonah, we have wondered why we don't get what we want when we've done what God wants. When we read this story, we are reading the story of a man of God who becomes angry at God's grace.

After the exciting part about the whale, our text for this morning moves to Jonah's arrival into Nineveh to deliver the message. There's good and bad news for the folks in Ninevah. The good news is that the message is short. The bad news is that the end for them is near. Jonah arrives and delivers his terse message with no words of consolation or advice, no call to repentance or confession. Instead, Jonah says, "Forty days more, and Nineveh shall be overthrown."

I understand, we all appreciate a short sermon. He is straight to the point. The question is, where did Jonah get that sermon? Immediately before the verses we read today, God says, "Proclaim the message that I tell you." But that is not what Jonah did.

How do I know? Well, I don't know exactly what God said to Jonah. But I know what God didn't say. He did not say, "Tell the people I'm going to destroy them and there's nothing they can do about it."

How do I know? I know because God doesn't say things like that. Oh, there have been times where prophets and people have been confused about how God speaks and what God says. It can be hard to discern and understand. Sometimes God shouts and sometimes God whispers. But if you look at the whole of scripture, God is constantly calling people into repentance so they can be reconciled and restored and redeemed. That is the work of God in the world.

The problem is that Jonah was focused on the destruction of Nineveh and he was unconcerned about the fate of the people.

We are always in trouble when we lose sight of people, when we get too wrapped up in power or politics, policies or problems. We forget that it is really about people.

Now, in Jonah's defense, let me say that Nineveh was a city that was deserving of God's judgment. Nineveh was the capital city of the Neo-Assyrian empire whose brutality was renowned. Violence was an art form for the Assyrians. Torture was not only tolerated, but advocated. Battles ended with brutal massacres. Jonah understood the Assyrian evil because the Hebrew people had been impacted by it. It was the Assyrians who had ordered the absolute annihilation of the Northern Kingdom of Israel. The Hebrews had been divided into 12 tribes and the Assyrians had destroyed 10 of them.

To appreciate Jonah's passion, we need to remember our own feelings in the wake of 9/11 toward Osama Bin Laden and Al-Qaeda. Jonah had these same feelings toward the city of Nineveh and the Assyrian empire. His people had been unjustly attacked. The Assyrians had killed the innocent. Jonah just wants the evil to be punished. He actually takes pleasure in delivering this message about their impending doom.

Before we judge Jonah too quickly, we need to recognize that in a similar situation, we might have the same feelings. We might take great pleasure in the demise and destruction of our enemies. We too might want to unleash God's wrath on those who have hurt us.

Jonah offers this short sermon about God's judgment and, much to his shock, the people of Nineveh listen and respond with repentance. He didn't even offer an invitation. No singing of "Just As I Am." The people respond anyway, confessing their sins. The King of Nineveh makes a proclamation that extends not only to all the people, but even to the livestock. People and animals were to fast and cover themselves with sackcloth as a sign of sorrow. The entire nation turns from its wicked ways.

Now, you would think, Jonah would be overjoyed. What preacher would not like to have an entire city respond to the altar call? But, instead, Jonah is filled with anger.

Our text tells us that when God saw what they did, how they turned from their wicked ways, God changed his mind about the calamity.

The people of Nineveh became recipients— not of God's wrath, but rather of God's grace. God sometimes changes. We rarely talk about this, but in the Old Testament, this action occurs over and over again. Scriptures are not embarrassed to say that God changes God's mind. We see examples of it in Exodus, Samuel, Amos, Hosea and here in Jonah. God changes God's mind.

There is a lesson here for us. If God changes God's mind, we should not be afraid to change our own minds on this journey through life. Do you know some of the saddest people? They are those who have never changed. They are trapped in the past. They have not grown because growth requires change. The only things that are not growing are dead.

As a father, I love my children, where they are and as they are. But I also want them to grow, to mature, to stop talking so much when we are taking trips; in short, to change.

It was the Apostle Paul who said, *When I was a child, I spoke like a child, I thought like a child, I reasoned like a child; but then I became an adult.*

Do you know where you find these verses? They are in 1 Corinthians 13—the "Love Chapter." Do you know why? Because love changes.

Last August, my parents celebrated their 50th wedding anniversary. Much to my surprise, my father, an engineer and salesman, turned into a poet. He wrote this amazing poem and read it to my Mom in front of all of us. It was called, "Seasons of Marriage."

I won't read it all, but let me tell you a little about what it said:

"In Spring, the excitement of dating and the first kiss on the front porch.
In Summer, life is filled with activities— jobs, sports, the first day of school and off to college.
In Autumn, a time to enjoy being with each other and to pass on some of what we have learned.
Winter will come when we can't travel; our steps are slower.
But winter is filled with beauty as well."

Do you know what that poem is really about? It's about how love changes.

How do we know God changes? Because God is love.

God changes God's mind. However, God does not change God's nature. Rather, in response to people and to being in relationship with people, it becomes necessary for God to follow a different line of action in order to be true to the nature of God. God's nature is just, but also merciful. God's nature is fierce, but also forgiving. For in God, the law and love are fully reconciled. It is a different way of being. The way of God is the way of Grace.

Jonah was angry because God had forgiven his enemies. The sight of thousands of Assyrians repenting and turning to God enraged him. Jonah was angry that God chose to have compassion on the heathen as well as on the Hebrews. Jonah was angry because he wanted to see God's wrath unleashed—not God's grace bestowed. Jonah was angry because he knew God's nature.

Jonah said, "I knew you were a gracious and merciful God, slow to anger, and abounding in steadfast love, and ready to relent from punishing." Jonah knew what God was like. Jonah just didn't like it.

We see glimpses of this anger in other places in the scriptures. We find this same resentful anger in the story of the prodigal son. You remember it, right? When the prodigal returns, his elder brother stands in the shadows and watches his father extend grace to his younger brother. The elder brother responds with anger and hate that his father did not react with wrath and punishment.

Jonah was like that elder brother. Sometimes, we may feel the same way. We want a person to get what is coming to them. We may talk about grace on Sunday mornings, but when we leave the worship service, we are far more concerned with fairness. We hold grudges. We want to get back at those who have hurt us. When we look at our enemies, we want them to fail. We quietly celebrate when they do so. Like Jonah, we would rather watch God pour out God's wrath on our enemies than see them repent. When we embrace this attitude, we become dangerously close to rejecting the God of grace.

When we focus on what we perceive as the evil of others, we are often blind to our own sins and unable to recognize our own need for God's grace. We see something similar taking place in this story. Did you notice? It never even crossed Jonah's mind that though he may have been disobedient to God's command, God had pursued him with persistent love.

It never crossed Jonah's mind that if God were unforgiving, God would have let him drown in the storm. It never crossed Jonah's mind that the pagans on the ship, in their attempts to save his life, were more like God than he was.

It never seemed to cross Jonah's mind that even the fish was more obedient to God than he was. At least the fish, when commanded by God to vomit him up, did as it was told. Jonah, when commanded by God, did the opposite. Yet, God extended grace and pursued Jonah with love.

At the end of the story, as recorded in chapter four, Jonah wanders to a hillside. He is still holding out hope that he might see the destruction of Nineveh. It's as if he wants to get the best seat possible, so he goes to the front row of the balcony. God sends a bush to provide some shade from the punishing sun for his sulking prophet—but also to teach an important lesson. The next morning, the same bush is attacked by a worm and withers away.

Jonah reacts dramatically with anger. He declares that he would just rather be dead.

The story doesn't have a happy ending, at least not for Jonah. The people of Nineveh are spared. God's grace is extended. But Jonah is still bitter.

God asks a question, "You were concerned about the bush. It came into being in the night and it perished in the night. And it's just a bush! Should I not be concerned about Nineveh, a city of 120,000 persons? Should I not be concerned about them?"

Jonah never answers. He is left brooding in the hot sun, consumed with anger.

God asks us today, "Should I not be concerned about them—be they Republican or Democrat; be they conservative or liberal; be they old or young; be they married or single or unwed or widowed; be they black or white; be they citizen or non-citizen immigrants; be they gay or straight; be they rich or poor; be they police or protestors; be they Baptists, Methodists, or Catholics; be they Buddhists, Muslims or Jews?"

And again God asks, "Should I not be concerned about them?"

What happens with Jonah? We don't know. But I know this: You are sitting in the choir loft, or in your home, or in the "shade" of your couch. And you think about those people you dislike, those people you consider to be your opponents or your enemies, those who annoy you or anger you every time you see their faces or hear their voices.

And God says, "Should I not be concerned about them?"

And God says, "Should *you* not be concerned about them?"

So, Jonah was first and foremost a recipient of God's grace. But he never really knew it. Friends, you and I are recipients of God's grace. Open your eyes. Recognize it. Realize it. And then extend it to others.

God waited for Jonah to answer. And now God is waiting for us.

Let's pray.

A Different Way of Teaching

*They went to Capernaum; and when the
sabbath came, he entered the synagogue and
taught.*

*They were astounded at his teaching, for he
taught them as one having authority, and not
as the scribes. Just then there was in their
synagogue a man with an unclean spirit, and
he cried out, "What have you to do with us,
Jesus of Nazareth? Have you come to
destroy us? I know who you are, the Holy
One of God." But Jesus rebuked him, saying,
"Be silent, and come out of him!" And the
unclean spirit, throwing him into convulsions
and crying with a loud voice, came out of
him. They were all amazed, and they kept on
asking one another, "What is this? A new
teaching—with authority! He commands
even the unclean spirits, and they obey him."
At once his fame began to spread throughout
the surrounding region of Galilee.*

-Mark 1:21-28, NRSV

The scriptures tell us *"they went to
Capernaum,"* which was Jesus' adopted
hometown.

If you ever visit Israel, you will discover that Capernaum is now a ghost town. You can see a few ruins, but no one lives there. Now, lest you get confused, Capernaum was never really more than what we might call a "hole in the wall." When you hear about it being Jesus' hometown, you might imagine something grand and great. It was the center of Jesus' ministry. But, in truth, it was really just a little fishing village that was easy to overlook. It would not even be noted on most maps.

In many ways, it would be the least likely place to find the Son of God.

Have you ever heard of Mound City, Illinois? Of course, you haven't. It is northwest of Cairo and southwest of Carbondale. It is on the banks of the Mississippi River, smack dab in the middle of nowhere. My great uncle, a World War II veteran and one of my heroes, grew up there.

A few years back, my Uncle Tom took me to see his hometown. He would say, "Look, Chris, over there, that's where the farm was." And there was nothing there. A little further, "That's where we had a store." And again, there was nothing there. Just a few buildings that were falling apart was all that was left of this community.

In some ways, Capernaum is the same way today. One of the few remaining structures are the stone steps to the synagogue. Archeologists believe these steps were there when Jesus lived and worked and ministered. One of these stones may have been the very step upon which Jesus walked in the story that we read today.

There is Jesus, in this little village of Capernaum, doing what he always does — going to synagogue. He doesn't make a splash. At this point, we are still in the first chapter of Mark's Gospel. It's early in Jesus' recorded ministry. No one even seems to know who Jesus is. He is just another Jew at the synagogue.

The story sounds absolutely, well, ordinary... and dare I even say it? It sounds boring. (Is it okay to say that the Bible is boring sometimes? I didn't get an "amen" from the choir, but I know I could have.)

Then, Jesus starts teaching. And people's ears start to perk up. "Wait a minute! Who is this guy?"

It reminds me of when I came to Smoke Rise almost eight years ago, believe it or not. For the first few months, I focused on preaching. I did not do any teaching until about six months after my arrival. On that first Wednesday night in August when I taught a Bible study, going verse-by-verse, trying to help people to see the text and the context, I was really enjoying myself. After it was over, someone came and said, "Wow! I am surprised. You are a good teacher!"

I responded, "I know. It's a shocker, right?"

They said the same thing to Jesus, "Wow! You're a good teacher!" This may have been the first time Jesus taught in Capernaum and the people are surprised. Scripture tells us, "He taught as one having authority."

Don't you wish you could have been a fly on the wall? I wonder *what* he was teaching. I wonder *how* he was teaching. What was the text for that Sabbath Day? What did he say? If you could have been there, would you have been impressed?

It is hard to impress us now. We have TED talks. We have social media posts. We have 24-hour news. We have Twitter. We can watch videos on Facebook about cats climbing up trees or a little baby bird in the nest. Now, that's all entertainment. But when it comes to a sermon, it's hard to impress.

I remember my son David saying to me one day, "Daddy, I like it when you preach."

Well, I was touched until he said, "But I like it best when it is over."

Now, Jesus is preaching and teaching, and that's fine. But what happens when a person possessed by an unclean spirit shows up in the synagogue. Jesus doesn't miss a beat. He shouts, "Be silent and come out of him!" The man convulses and the unclean spirit leaves him.

Of course, the people are amazed and rightly so. They are suddenly sitting on the edge of their seats. The men who were almost asleep wake up. Kids are standing on tippy toes to see what's happening.

There is part of the text that I had never noticed before. Look closely and you will see something strange. As Jesus taught, the people were amazed and kept asking, "What is this? A new teaching with authority."

He had just performed an exorcism and they are still talking about his teaching. That's amazing. He had just performed a miracle. Incredible! People should have been pointing their fingers, overwhelmed by what they saw, and what Jesus did. But instead, they were still talking about his words, his teaching with authority.

What does it mean to teach with authority and why was it so amazing?

At first, I didn't understand. Then, I remembered someone. His name was Dub Edwards, Dr. Dub Edwards. You probably have never heard of him. Some would say he was just ordinary, maybe at times even a bit boring.

When I was a high school senior, looking at colleges, I wanted to find a good Baptist school where I could learn to be a preacher. I heard about Samford University. I was talking with a minister friend of mine at my church, who was a caring and loving person, but who was concerned that Samford might be a little too liberal for me. I really didn't understand. I was not well-versed in all the theological battles that were raging in Southern Baptist life. I was just a kid, a teenager who didn't really want to stand up or to stand out, but just to fade into the woodwork of faith.

This minister told me, "Chris, I want you to go to Samford and I want you to march into the Religion Department. I want you to find a professor and I want you to ask them one question."

Well, friends, I was taking notes; my eyes were wide open.

This minister said, "You ask that professor, 'Do you believe in the inerrancy of scripture?'"

I said, "I don't even know what that means."

He answered, "It doesn't matter. The professor will. So, you ask, 'Do you believe in the inerrancy of scripture?' And if they say YES, you go to Samford. And if they say NO, you get away as fast as you can."

So, armed with my question as if it were a bullet in a gun, I went to the religion department. I found an unsuspecting victim, er, I mean professor, and fired my shot across the bow. "Do you believe in the inerrancy of scripture?"

And Dub Edwards looked up from his desk and said, "No. I don't."

Well, I knew I was supposed to run, but he caught me off guard when he said, "But, if you have a minute, sit down and let me tell you what I do believe about the Bible."

He proceeded to tell me that he read that Bible every day and that the Bible was the guidebook for his life. He told me he loved the Bible with all of his heart and all of his mind, and that's why he had dedicated his life to the study of it. He spoke of the texts with a tenderness I had not seen before, even from the pulpit. And he even read one of the Psalms as an example to me. I couldn't be sure, but it looked like there was a tear in his eye as he did so.

After about a half hour of his talking, Dub Edwards said, "So, I don't believe the Bible is inerrant, but I know it is inspired and I know that it inspires me. And I hope you will come to Samford."

I enrolled the following week. I took classes from Dub Edwards—I guess, because I sensed that he taught with authority and with humility. He didn't pretend to have all the answers. He had the courage to ask questions *with* us, his students. He helped me learn that the Bible was more than a bullet to be fired. It was a book to be read, studied, and treasured.

This teacher changed my life. I didn't have an unclean spirit, just an unconsidered faith. It was really nothing short of a miracle. I was amazed at his teaching.

Do you know what I think teaching with authority looks like? It is when what you say lines up with what you do. It is when you practice what you preach.

Do you know what amazed those crowds as Jesus taught? I think it was both what Jesus said and what Jesus did. The principles Jesus taught were the same principles that Jesus embodied. This meant that even his very life was the lesson. He was doing more than merely talking. He was always teaching.

We are too. Did you know? People are watching. Parents, your children are watching you. Grandparents, your grandchildren are watching you. Your friends and your neighbors, your coworkers and your classmates, they're watching you. They know you go to church on Sundays. That's ordinary; maybe some would even say boring.

They are interested in what happens *after* church. They are watching to see if what you say is reflected in what you do. And sadly, this is rare, so rare in our world.

The Bible says, "*Blessed are the peacemakers*;" but people are quick to pick fights and to level accusations in the news or social media. The Bible says, "*Love your neighbor;*" but people treat those with whom they disagree as enemies, labeling them instead of loving them.

What if we practiced common decency, showed gracious humility and extended kindness and love? I'm convinced, this is how we change the world. This is how we cast out the unclean spirits. We listen and learn; we preach and we teach. How we practice our faith, how we live out God's love and how we extend God's grace determines whether or not when we speak, we speak with authority.

Listen. One day, someone will say, "You have never heard of this place called Smoke Rise Baptist Church or Lilburn or Snellville or Decatur. But I need to tell you about someone who lived there, a person who shaped my life. It was not just what she said, it was what she did. It wasn't just his talk, but his actions. I never really considered him to be a teacher; he didn't have that title. How much I learned from her. Most folks have never heard of this person, but I will never forget

_____."

And then, they will say your name. I just know...they will say your name.

Let's pray.

A Different Way of Waiting

Have you not known? Have you not heard?
The Lord is the everlasting God,
  the Creator of the ends of the earth.
He does not faint or grow weary;
  his understanding is unsearchable.
He gives power to the faint,
  and strengthens the powerless.
Even youths will faint and be weary,
  and the young will fall exhausted;
but those who wait for the Lord shall renew
their strength,
  they shall mount up with wings like eagles,
they shall run and not be weary,
  they shall walk and not faint.

-Isaiah 40:29-31, NRSV

That evening, at sunset, they brought to him
all who were sick or possessed with demons.
And the whole city was gathered around the
door. And he cured many who were sick with
various diseases, and cast out many demons;
and he would not permit the demons to
speak, because they knew him.

In the morning, while it was still very dark,
he got up and went out to a deserted place,
and there he prayed. And Simon and his
companions hunted for him. When they

53

found him, they said to him, "Everyone is
searching for you." He answered, "Let us go
on to the neighboring towns, so that I may
proclaim the message there also; for that is
what I came out to do."

-Mark 1:32-38, NRSV

As the old saying goes, there are only two
kinds of people in the world. Some would say
male and females, or Christians and non-
Christians, or Republicans and Democrats.
Some in this section of the country tend to
think in terms of Yankees and Southerners.

But, in my thinking, the two kinds of people
are patient people and impatient people. My
wife is patient. I am impatient. Need
evidence? Just take a car ride with us. I will
get there sooner, but she will get you there
feeling a lot safer. In Atlanta, I think the
impatient people outnumber the patient
people.

Waiting is something that most endure, but
few enjoy. We don't have time to stop or to
wait.

When I was in high school, the country band
Alabama had memorable song called, "I'm in a
Hurry." The chorus goes like this:

I'm in a hurry to get things done,
I rush and rush until life's no fun.
All I really gotta' do is live and die
But I'm in a hurry and don't know why.

We all know the feeling. That's why today's scripture readings sound foreign and alien to our experience. The prophet Isaiah is talking about those who "wait for the Lord." Who is he talking about? I don't know those folks.

We don't even want to wait for food. That's why we go to Chick-Fil-A. The drive-through is like the fast lane; it may be looped around it four times but getting our food still takes only 15 minutes.

Spiritually speaking, if God is God, why do we have to wait?

Google gives us an instant response. We are conditioned to expect immediate answers. We have come to "feel the need for speed." And so speed is being sold to us; it is marketed. Your smartphone will soon be a 5-G phone, replacing the 4-G. Now my son David, who is all into electronics, asked me the other day, "Dad, are you so old..." (which is a bad way to start a question) "that you remember 3-G?" My answer: "Son, I remember when there were NO Gs anywhere!" We need speed.

And, sadly, it has come at a price in that sometimes we value fast more than fact. Our society would rather be quick and get it wrong, then wait to get it right. It happens to everyone, preachers included.

I am reminded of the story of Phillip Brooks, one of America's great preachers, who occupied the prestigious pulpit at Trinity Church in Copley Square in Boston. One afternoon, he was walking through the halls of the church looking frustrated and agitated. Because he was normally very jovial, everyone noticed. Finally, someone asked him if anything was wrong. He paused for a moment and said, "The trouble is that I am in a hurry, but God isn't."

What if finding truth takes time? What if we have to stop, before we go? What if God isn't bound by our scheduling conflicts? What if God wants us to wait?

If what we read in the prophet Isaiah isn't strange enough, there is the account of Jesus in Mark's Gospel. At first, as recorded in our Scripture reading today, he is doing exactly what he should be doing. He is busy. Mark tells us they brought to him all who were sick and possessed by demons and he cured them, all of them. He was doing real ministry and real work. It was a PR success as well, because we read that, "*The whole city gathered around the door.*"

Now that is familiar to us. Busier is better. Do Something.

But just when Jesus is getting successful, when the crowds are gathering around him, Jesus steps away. We read that, "*In the morning, while it was still very dark, he got up and went out to a deserted place to pray.*" To do what? To pray and to wait as if that's what he needed most to do in this moment.

His disciples are looking for him. They don't understand. They are thinking he was just "hitting his stride." They are saying, "Jesus, you can't slow down now; you can't stop. What are you waiting for?"

And what if Jesus' answer is, "God. I'm waiting for God. I'm here to speak and to listen."

There is wisdom in waiting. Are you willing to wait for God?

Catholic Theologian Henri Nouwen writes, "The mystery of work, and the mystery of love, and the mystery of friendship, and the mystery of community—they all involve waiting. And that is the mystery of Jesus' love. God reveals himself in Jesus as one who waits. And precisely in that waiting the intensity of God's love is revealed for us."

God's calling is for us to wait patiently. It is not to annoy or irritate us. We wait patiently because it helps us to better imitate Jesus. God could do in a moment what it takes us weeks or months to do. But God waits. God honors us by waiting for us. And we honor God by waiting for God.

Waiting may not be easy. However, somewhere along the way, we discover that those difficult times of waiting are the same times in which our faith grows stronger and our vision becomes clearer. We acquire not only patience, but also gain perspective.

I am still learning the importance of patience. My four-year-old daughter, Emma Pearl, is a good teacher. Since her legs are much shorter than mine, when we go for a walk, I have a terrible tendency to get a few steps ahead of her. She will call out, "Wait for me, Daddy! Wait for me." And when I stop, when I wait, I look back at this little miracle—this little girl who wants more than anything in the world just to hold my hand and walk beside me. In that instant, I remember what matters and what doesn't. It's easy to lose sight of those things when we are busy. But when we wait, we can see again what is important.

In this season, in this year of Covid, some of us are growing impatient with waiting. I understand. Patience is a virtue I don't possess. But I'm learning. This often is the wisdom that comes with waiting.

God has this wonderful way of using the waiting places in our lives—the places others might consider the wastelands—to work in us. The waiting places are not just periods of stillness and stagnation, but more often are times of significant personal growth. Waiting may be the process that God uses to reshape our lives and sharpen our vision.

If Jesus needed to step away, to wait, certainly you and I need to wait too. Why? *Because those who wait on the Lord shall renew their strength...*

You see, waiting is actually an exercise in humility. If we believe everything depends exclusively on us, we had better get busy. But if we believe that we are meant to depend on God and others, we had better learn to wait.

We also need to recognize that waiting is not always a burden, but is often a blessing. If we see life as a gift from God, waiting can be an act of obedience and worship.

Sometimes, at the end of one's life's journey, when all has been said that needs to be said and when all has been done that needs to be done, there is nothing else to do but wait. And so, family and friends gather around their loved one, at a hospice facility or at home. More often than not, those rooms are filled not only with tears, but also with laughter and lots and lots of stories. Because in those rooms, we remember things we had once known, but had almost forgotten, things we haven't talked about in years and years. So we wait together. It is about more than a just a point in time, it is about our perception of time itself. It's a recognition that life is a gift.

So, don't just look at your watch. Don't just stare at your smartphone. Look UP. God calls us to wait differently. *"Those who wait...shall renew their strength...they shall mount up with wings like eagles, they shall run and not be weary, they shall walk and not faint."*

God wants us to wait, because God wants us to ultimately soar. We engage in the process of waiting so that we can be empowered to walk, and to run, and to rise.

Jesus waited. Then he said to the disciples, "Let's go to the neighboring towns so I can proclaim the message, so I can preach and teach, help and heal, care and share. That's what I came here to do."

Three verses later, we read that Jesus is healing a leper. Ten verses later, we see Jesus healing a paralyzed man.

Jesus waited patiently, so that he could then go and minister passionately. Jesus waited patiently so that he would gain a new perspective and see the bigger picture.

We can so easily get lost or overwhelmed in any moment; but waiting causes us to step back to see things more clearly.

Waiting isn't easy. It requires us to give up our most precious treasure, our time. Or, perhaps, it is not so much giving it up as investing it well and wisely.

Before James Garfield became president of the United States, he was president of Hiram College in Ohio. A male student there was failing a course. His father, a generous donor to the school, met with Garfield to ask if a particular course of study couldn't be simplified so that his son could go through by a shorter route. "It would save time," the man argued.

"Certainly, it is possible," Garfield replied. "But it all depends upon what you want to make of your son. When God wants to make an oak tree, it takes a hundred years. When God wants to make a squash, it only requires a few weeks one summer."

Waiting makes us a certain kind of people. When we offer God our time, we offer God our treasure and God takes this gift and redeems it. We bring God our patience and God offers us a new perspective so that we can see and become all that God created us to be.

Now, I know that some of you are thinking, "I can't wait for this sermon to be over."

Well, it is.

A Different Way of Wandering

But he himself went a day's journey into the wilderness, and came and sat down under a solitary broom tree. He asked that he might die: "It is enough; now, O Lord, take away my life, for I am no better than my ancestors." Then he lay down under the broom tree and fell asleep. Suddenly an angel touched him and said to him, "Get up and eat." He looked, and there at his head was a cake baked on hot stones, and a jar of water. He ate and drank, and lay down again. The angel of the Lord came a second time, touched him, and said, "Get up and eat, otherwise the journey will be too much for you." He got up, and ate and drank; then he went in the strength of that food for forty days and forty nights to Horeb the mount of God.

-1 Kings 19:4-8, NRSV

You have probably never heard of Max Bond, but you've seen his work.

Let's start a little earlier. Max Bond was a successful student, any doubt of that vindicated by his admittance into Harvard University. In the 1950's, while some were still openly questioning the intellectual capacity of African Americans, Bond had demonstrated an ability to excel academically and overcome obstacles. Despite all of his achievements, some people were still openly hostile toward him.

During his first semester at Harvard, a cross was burned in front of his freshman dorm. Instead of responding with outrage toward the perpetrators, Harvard's administration threatened Max with suspension if he reported the incident to the Boston newspapers. When Max expressed interest in architecture as a career, one of his professors told him there was no place for a black man in architecture. Another professor trashed his design, then fed his idea to a white student.

Bond felt isolated and ostracized, persecuted and threatened. He must have struggled with doubt and depression and battled against a mental breakdown. Sitting in his dorm room, he must have wondered, "Why am I here? What can I do?"

Elijah was clearly a successful prophet who was vindicated by his incredible victory over the priests of Baal on Mount Carmel. That story precedes the verses we read today. In an amazing made-for-television contest to see whose god would consume the offering on the altar, Elijah prayed to God and the priests prayed to Baal. Everyone else watched to see who would win.

The priests of Baal prayed to their god and failed. In a short and eloquent prayer, Elijah asked for his God to come to his aid. Seconds later, fire fell down from heaven, consuming not only Elijah's offering, but the entire altar. And while the crowds cheered the victory, King Ahab and Queen Jezebel were unimpressed. They pledged to destroy the prophet, promising to take his life to avenge the prophets of Baal.

Elijah did what anyone would do confronted with this situation. He ran. In our text today, we read that he stops running and sits down in the shade. He must have felt isolated and ostracized, persecuted and threatened. He must have struggled with doubt and despair. Sitting under the broom tree, he wondered, *"Why am I here? What can I do?"*

While we may not have the same experiences as Bond or Elijah, all of us have at some moment struggled with this same despair and asked these same questions. We have grown weary trying to do the right things, only to experience more obstacles and feel threatened by the world around us. We do the right

things but get the wrong results. We may
have gifts, talents and abilities, but how
quickly we forget any of our successes in the
midst of struggles. We work hard. We pray
hard. But, still, in the back of our minds, we
wonder if we will ever reach the promised
land. If we will ever get THERE.

When we have these feelings, we join others
walking in the wilderness.

Our text for today says that *"Elijah went a
day's journey into the wilderness, and came
and sat down under a solitary broom tree."*

We know the wilderness as a dangerous place
that supports little life. The wilderness is
never anyone's destination. It is kind of like
Arkansas. We travel through it, but not to it.
We stay in the wilderness only when
absolutely necessary, when we have no other
choice. Perhaps when the car breaks down.

Or, we go to our doctor's appointment and get
that diagnosis that shatters our hopes and
dreams. We don't ever plan to go there; we
don't want to be there. But once we find our
way in, it's hard to get out. The feelings that
led us into the wilderness—the fear, the
fatigue, and the despair make it almost

impossible for us to find the strength to leave that desolate setting.

The wilderness is also hot and humid. Imagine summer in Atlanta, or better yet, imagine summer in New Orleans. I lived in New Orleans as a child. What do I remember? Beignets. Because I was a child that loved sugar. But beyond beignets, I remember that it was hot, so hot. And it was humid, miserably humid.

Elijah arrives in the wilderness and, like any good Southerner, immediately looks for shade. He finds a broom tree, which is really less like a tree and more like a large bush. And apparently, the shade offers very little comfort. In fact, Elijah is so hot that he asks God to let him die.

God listens to Elijah in the wilderness just as God listens to us in the wilderness. Elijah didn't get what he asked for. We may not get what we ask for either. Sometimes, God answers with silence.

As a pastor, I have talked with many people who have struggled in the wilderness with God's silence. Many of you know that my wife was a pediatric nurse and, in her role, Jen frequently interacted with families who were enduring this silence. Chaplains in hospitals see the suffering of people dealing with a terminal diagnosis and families who are seeking answers to their questions. People have prayed over and over again. Pastors and parents, family and friends, doctors and nurses have prayed. Sometimes, those prayers are answered by a miraculous intervention. There is no other explanation. But, other times, the prayers seem to go unanswered. Parents confess their confusion and their anger with a God that seems to be silent in the midst of their suffering.

God's silence is never easy to endure. Elijah wonders if God is even listening as he lies there in the shade.

But our story doesn't end with the silence. After the silence, exhausted by his experiences, Elijah falls asleep and finds rest. In his slumber, something unexpected happens. God changes the wilderness from a hot and humid and hard place into something sacred and holy. God does not provide an explanation, but offers words of encouragement. God does not alter the situation, but supplies the strength to endure in the midst of the struggle.

God transforms this stopping point into a starting point. Elijah had prayed for his own death. God answered, "No." After the silence, clearly God does not answer Elijah's prayer for death. Instead, God offers him a new life. An angel visits Elijah, bringing food and water. God tells him, *"Get up; eat. Otherwise, the journey will be too much for you."*

Elijah was to keep wandering, keep going. It was J.R.R. Tolkien who wrote in *The Fellowship of the Rings*, "Not all those who wander are lost...And from the ashes a fire shall be woken, A light from the shadows shall spring."

This is what God says to Elijah, who feels lost as if he's lying on a pile of ashes. God says, "Get up. Your journey is not over. Get up. I have a plan for your life. Get up. I have somewhere for you to go and something for you to do. *Get up. Eat. Get ready."*

Friends, there is a time to wait, as we talked about last week. But there is also a time to get up and to go.

Something amazing happened in Elijah's story. God met Elijah in the wilderness. And I believe God will meet us in the wilderness as well. All of us will have to walk in the wilderness at some point. We all know that experience. We long to get out and we feel hungry. We struggle with how to move forward. But if we have the courage to carry on, we will discover that God will provide strength for our journey. And God will call out to each of us, "Get up. Eat. Journey on."

Max Bond heard that calling. Sitting in his dorm room at Harvard, he made a choice to carry on, to complete his education. In fact, he graduated early from Harvard University, then finished his master's degree in architecture, despite what everyone was telling him. He went on to design buildings in France, Ghana and New York. He designed the Civil Rights Museum in Birmingham and the Martin Luther King, Jr., Center for Non-Violent Social Change here in Atlanta. In his last project, he helped to design the National September 11th Memorial and Museum at the World Trade Center. He passed in February 2009. Thank God, when things got hard, he kept walking through the wilderness.

Elijah heard that calling. His story did not end in the wilderness. He took up his mantle, regained his courage and followed God's calling.

I don't know where you are this morning. But I know that at least a few folks who can hear my voice—a few feel as though they are wandering in the wilderness. They don't know when they will get out. I know some who hear my voice are experiencing the silence of God. Some may be struggling with doubt or depression or despair.

The Good News of the Gospel is that wherever you are, whoever you are, whatever you may have done, God knows you. And God loves you. And God will meet you in the middle of your wilderness. Because, for God, sometimes the destination IS the wilderness. And in that place, God touches us through angelic and human hands, and brings us hope and strength for the journey.

Frederick Buechner said, "Here in the world, beautiful and terrible things will happen. Don't be afraid."

And God says to you, "Get up. Your journey is not over. Get up. Go."

Let's pray.

About the Author:

Chris George is the Senior Pastor at Smoke Rise Baptist Church in Georgia, a position he has held since April 2013. Before coming to Georgia, Chris served as the Pastor of First Baptist Church of Mobile, Alabama. He has served congregations in Georgia, Kentucky, Massachusetts, and Virginia. He received a Doctor of Ministry degree from Methodist Theological School of Ohio with a dissertation focused on the power of story to foster community. He has a Master of Theology degree in Christianity and Culture from Harvard Divinity School and a Bachelor of Arts degree from Samford University.

Chris has been married for sixteen years to his wife, Jen. They are the proud parents of four children: David, Evan, Andy, and Emma Pearl who keep them busy, blessed, and stressed in every strange season of life.

Chris finds inspiration for writing from his family and friends as well as the scripture, the Spirit, and several cups of coffee a day. Among his great loves are Kentucky basketball, jellybeans, and planning his family's next great adventure.

Chris preaches weekly at Smoke Rise Baptist Church, and regularly offers bible studies. Visit www.smokerisebaptist.org to follow his preaching and teaching.

Made in the USA
Columbia, SC
04 March 2021